A PRACTICAL GUIDE TO SPIRITUAL AWARENESS

THE PROCESS

PAIN, FORGIVENESS, AND PEACE

Bre W

WISEPRODUCTIONS PUBLISHING

CHICAGO, IL

The Process

Unless otherwise noted, all Scripture quotations are taken from the HOLY BIBLE, New International Version. NIV

Verses marked ESV are taken from English Standard Version Published in 2001 by Crossway

Verses marked KJV are taken from early modern English translation of the Christian Bible Published in 1611 By Sponsorship of King James Version @wikisource

Verses marked NLT are taken from New Living Translation Published in 1996 by Tyndale House Foundation Created by 90 leading bible scholars

Verses marked NRSV are taken from New Revised Standard Version Translation of the Bible in contemporary English. Published in 1989 by National Council of the Churches of Christ in the USA

Copyright © 2023 by Breonna Ward

Published by Wiseproductions LLC

Chicago, Il 60643

Cover Illustration: BreW

Cover Design: BreW

Library of Congress Cataloging-in-Publication Data

ISBN: 978-1-962849-45-6

Printed in the USA

DEDICATION

This book is dedicated to all who have been affected by or are still going through an unbalanced phase of life and are looking for tools to navigate obstacles, trials, turmoil, and uncertainties.

In loving memory.

I love you Sis(Alexis) you're forever missed.

Table Of Contents

FOREWORD

Breonna is my mother, friend, nurturer, advisor, and, most importantly, the person whom I have grown to love each day more and more. I have seen my mom grow into an awesome parent, daughter, caring sister, wife, friend, and boss to so many people that it's unbelievable she hasn't lost her mind. She put in so much hard work and time in writing this book. I know without a doubt it will help many people. The passion my mom has for God and wanting to see others live a joy-filled life shows me how she can operate at the capacity she does. I have seen and heard this book's chapters spoken in our household. I've seen my mom's interaction with God, herself, and others. My mom has a gift she probably didn't realize she had because it comes naturally to her to speak life into others and think about others before thinking of herself.

As her daughter and sometimes her co-creator (I helped with the color choices and book cover ideas!), I believe my mom has made an outstanding choice in writing her first book titled *The Process* because she has experienced every bit of each chapter while instilling in me the same values.

I'm so very grateful to call her my mom!

PREFACE

The PROCESS was the start of my self-healing when I tried to cope with obstacles of my own without searching for answers from others. The PROCESS was developed by spending quiet time with God and having an excellent therapeutic counselor.

Therapy is one of the best sources for getting advice without feeling embarrassed or ashamed. I understood who I am and was, knowing that issues exist within myself but allowing myself to heal in a way that God wants healing and not my own understanding.

~ Proverbs 3:5~

INTRODUCTION

The **Process** *will give you clarity on how to walk through different phases of life with the understanding that you just need coping mechanisms and tools to handle all circumstances.*

The **Process** *will guide you to or get you closer to your spiritual side of life. This reading will hopefully give you some sense of purpose in life and help you gain consistency in your prayer life, overcome life struggles, and serve God.*

The **Process** *is your tool to help you gain access to your spiritual Father and help you to know the how in life.*

The **Navigation** *of life can be traumatic if you weren't taught or raised to know how to overcome difficult circumstances. Life can be overwhelming and cause you to take many steps back and routes that weren't designed for us to take.*

~ Romans 12:2 ~

I hope the **Process** *will help non-Christians and Christians. Christians at times struggle with a consistent prayer life; we have an unbalanced life, and we struggle with following the commandments, basically, all the chapters in this book, if not more.*

My prayer is that this book brings healing to what you might have not yet figured out; that this book will uplift your spirits, give you confidence, and restore what you thought you had once lost or couldn't control.

~ 1 John 5:4 ~

My prayer is that the **Process** *is meaningful to you, that it is easily understood, and it blesses you so much you can't put it down.*

~ Proverbs 11:25 ~

My **Prayer** *is that you find this book helpful and that you can forward it to others to help them through the same situations you have encountered.*

~ Hebrews 13:16 ~

To walk through life and not know your purpose or the purpose God has intended for you is unfulfilling, unproductive, and full of uncertainties. It comes with a tremendous amount of stress, health issues, mind-blowing situations, and depression.

—*Bre W*

1 Prayer

We cannot go through life without a prayer life. Prayer is the key to the longevity of everything we long for. I believe that people who don't maintain a consistent prayer life will live a more unbalanced life. To my knowledge and experience, we don't have to live a Christian, holier-than-thou lifestyle to pray.

Definition of prayer - a solemn request for the help or expression of thanks addressed to God or an object of worship.

Biblical Definition - a devout petition to God or an object of worship; a spiritual communion with God or an object of worship, as in supplication, thanksgiving, adoration, or confession; the act or practice of praying to God or an object of worship.

Jesus' Definition - a private time between God and the worshiper. Prayer should be sincere and with the right motives.

Keys to a Prayer Life:

Prayer is the key to our God or how we communicate with God, our Supreme higher being. Prayer is the master key, y'all!

1. Pray right – Pray for the things that will glorify the Lord. Unfortunately, the things we pray for are most of the time for ourselves. This is selfishness.

James 4: 2-3 (NLT) **You want what you don't have, so you scheme and kill to get it. You are jealous of what others have, but you can't** get it, so you fight and wage war to take it away from them. Yet you don't have what you want because you don't ask God for it. And even when you ask, you don't get it because your motives are all wrong--you want only what will give you pleasure.

2. Pray with confidence – We must believe that God hears us and will answer us.

John 5:14-15 (NLT) **And we are confident that he hears us whenever we ask for anything that pleases him. Since we know he hears us when we make our requests, we also know that he will give us what we ask for.**

3. Pray continuously - For anything to be effective, it needs consistency, especially prayer.

Thessalonians 5:17 (KJV) **Never stop praying.**

4. Pray with meditation - Joshua 1:8 (NLT) **Study this book of instructions continually. Meditate on it day and night so you will be sure to obey everything written in it; only then will you prosper and succeed in all you do.**

5. Pray with a righteous heart, be pure and authentic - Proverbs 15:29 (NLT)**The Lord is far from the wicked, but he hears the prayers of the righteous.**

6. Pray with expectations. Expect that God will give and do what you ask; as long as it is aligned with God's will and purpose - Matthew 7:7 (KJV) **Ask and it shall be given you; seek and ye shall find; knock and it shall be opened unto you.**

7. Pray specifically – Tell God what you want. Matthew 20:32- 34 (NLT) **When Jesus heard them, he stopped and called. "What do you want me to do for you?" "Lord," they said, "we want to see!" Jesus felt sorry for them and touched their eyes. Instantly, they could see! Then they followed him.**

It is my prayer that everyone who reads this book will either start or continue their journey by praying consistently.

~ Bre W ~

Journal page

2 Forgiveness

This may be the hardest chapter to either do or understand. A consistent prayer life will go hand in hand with this chapter. Please understand that forgiveness isn't for the person who needs forgiveness. (They will be accountable for their own actions.) Forgiveness is for you, your salvation, and God's glory!

Definition of **FORGIVENESS** - a conscious, deliberate decision to release feelings of resentment or vengeance toward a person or group who has harmed you, regardless of whether they deserve your forgiveness.

Biblical version - God's promise not to count our sins against us.

Matthew 6: 14-15 (NLT) **If you forgive those who sin against you, your heavenly father will forgive you. But if you refuse to forgive others, your father will not forgive you your sins.**

Jesus' Definition – Forgive others so you can be forgiven by God for your sins.

John 20:23 (NLT) **If you forgive anyone's sins, they are forgiven. If you do not forgive them, they are not forgiven.**

Forgiveness doesn't mean we let people get away with things, but more so, we let go of those feelings that come with a grudge towards a person. Feelings of hatred and anger can cause harm to the person feeling them.

The person who has done wrong must show remorse in a pleasant way, not in an egotistic or selfish way. The wrong person needs to pray to God and ask for forgiveness as well as to the person they have wronged.

Forgiving is something we're going to keep doing throughout our entire life. If you believe in our Lord and Savior Jesus Christ, it says:

"How many times must I forgive an offense?"

"Seventy times seven," Jesus said to Peter. (Matthew 18:21-22)

Please understand Jesus wasn't literally saying seventy times seven because that is only four hundred and ninety times. That would seem like forever in our human mind, but that's it! He literally meant to forgive a person as often as they need forgiveness, which could equate to forever or as often as they wrong us.

As I write this, it hit me hard because I know most of you who read this love the Lord and try to please him the best way we were taught (like in the Ten Commandments). We're disappointed in ourselves when we don't follow his instructions. It is common sense that if we follow his instructions, we shouldn't have a hard time forgiving and expressing love for one another. Since God gives grace and mercy, and forgives us, he also challenges us to forgive one another, which at times seems unbearable to do.

Keys to FORGIVENESS:

1. Understand what forgiveness means for you.

2. Stop being judgmental. Look in the mirror at your own faults and times when you need forgiveness.

3. Move forward in life. This means you don't need to be with that person or even socialize with them.

4. Address the inner pain.

5. Develop a mindset to forgive.

6. Try to NOT have any ill feelings, i.e., words, hatred, resentment, jealousy, etc. Any feeling that isn't pleasing to God.

7. Pray and forgive yourself!

Ephesians 4:32 **Be kind and compassionate to one another, forgiving each other, just as in Christ God forgave you.**

LETTING GO should be the new you.

LETTING GO should be the new practice.

You will know you have forgiven a person of an offense if you can see them, smile, and keep it moving. You can discuss the issue and not be triggered by the offense.

FYI—you haven't forgiven an offense if you constantly bring up the situation either to yourself (keeping pondering on it) or others, especially the person who has wronged you through arguments or nonargumentative conversation. Stop trying to figure out why they did what they did. The situation is done. Figure out the problem and resolve the issue so hopefully, it won't happen again.

Stop waiting for the next mess-up!!!!!

Allow Christ to set you free and live a happier and free life! God can and will set us free from our difficult situations; keep

trusting and having faith that God's will for us will be done. God will set us free by giving us eternal life during our sinful ways; long as we sincerely repent and not intentionally repeat our sin. It's our consistency that will lead to our determination; our determination will allow our repentance to flourish inside of us; that gives us the glory of eternal life God promised us.

~ Bre W ~

Journal page

3 Overcoming

To be a better version of oneself is to overcome setbacks that have caused a great deal of hurt, pain, trauma, and disappointment. Life is bittersweet more times than just sweet. What an awesome life we can live if we are able to overcome obstacles as soon as we encounter them. Life is designed to need God. If we stroll through life thinking we don't need God, we're up for a rude awakening.

Definition of **OVERCOME** - Success in dealing with a problem or difficulty.

Biblical definition - Deuteronomy 31:6 (NLT) **Be strong and courageous! Do not be afraid, and do not panic before them. For the Lord your God will personally go ahead of you. He will neither fail you nor abandon you.**

Jesus' Definition - John 16:33 (NLT) **I have told you all this so that you may have peace in me. Here on earth you will have many trials and sorrows. But take heart, because I have overcome the world." Jesus has overcome the world for us: so, remember to have peace because Jesus says to have peace, remember there will be tribulations. But go with hard times in good cheer because Jesus died for us to be at peace.**

Keys to **OVERCOME:**

1. Recognize the problem or issue.

2. Recognize the who or what of the issue.

3. Get help, counseling, or therapy.

4. Do not try to solve your own issues.

5. Seek God, go after God.

6. Do not stagnate on a problem.

7. Pray. Joshua 1:9 (NLT) **This is my command—be strong and courageous! Do not be afraid or discouraged. For the Lord your God is with you wherever you go."**

Prayer, forgiveness, and overcoming issues with resolutions will allow us to walk the path of peace.

~ Proverbs 3:16 -18 ~ NRSV

" Long life in her right hand; in her hand are riches and honor.

Her ways are ways of pleasantness, and all her paths are peace. She is a tree of life to those who lay hold of her; those who hold her fast are called blessed."

~ Proverbs 3:5 ~ NLT

Trust in the Lord with all your heart: do not depend on your own understanding. ~

Journal page

4 Unclean Spirit

There's nothing like having an unclean spirit. What is an unclean spirit? The things that come out our mouth from our heart, i.e....Suppose you have bitterness, unforgiveness, resentment, jealousy, evilness, hatred, retaliation, slander, gossip, stealing, lying, gossiping, hurtful ways, sexual sin, or any thought or act that's not pleasing to God. In that case, We cannot hold everyone around us accountable for our mishaps. Being wronged by someone isn't always the reason for people's unclean spirit; it could be what they've done to themselves or even regrets over bad decisions.

Definition of unclean spirit - a person considered extremely wicked, evil, or cruel.

Biblical definition - "unclean spirits," "impure spirits," "deceiving spirits," "lying spirits," "demonic spirits," and "demons." In all cases, evil spirits are malevolent supernatural beings. Evil spirits work against God, but the Bible also informs us that God in his sovereignty, can choose to use evil spirits to carry out his plans and purposes, demonstrating that he is ruler over all.

Jesus Definition - Matthew 12:26 **All manner of sin and blasphemy shall be forgiven unto men who receive me and repent but the blasphemy against the Holy Ghost, it shall not be forgiven unto men.**

Keys to release **Unclean spirits**:

1. Acknowledge unclean spirits that exist within you.

2. Realize that you can overcome this unclean spirit!

3. Have faith that this unclean spirit can be released.

4. Maintain consistency with your inner self.

5. Be persistent to work at getting better and healing.

6. Stay away from negativity.

7. Pray and seek God in all that you do.

Deuteronomy 33:27 (KJV) **The eternal God is thy refuge, and underneath are the everlasting arms, and he shall thrust out the enemy before thee; and shall say, destroy them.**

Releasing unwanted and unclean thoughts is what we need to experience more joy, happiness, peace, and the forgiveness that we all so yearn for and need from God. We can then deliver it to others for our soul, our healing, and our deliverance from God.

~Forgiveness is for us. ~

Journal page

5 Healing

The process of healing for me was letting go. Letting go doesn't mean forgetting; it shouldn't be for getting revenge and retaliation. Nor should we have negative thoughts about the person, situation, or thing that we need healing from. Healing will renew your thoughts and the way you react. Healing will leave you feeling refreshed. Never doubt the power of healing.

Here's a thought for you. If you've ever been cut or had a paper cut, the tenderness of that wound will make you cry. But with a little help of ointment and a Band-Aid, you will soon have some relief from pain. Healing takes time, with the help of God.

Definition of healing - the process of making or becoming sound or healthy again.

Biblical Definition – Healing occurs through the blending of forces that restore, transform, sustain, and nurture the whole person (body, mind, spirit) at each phase and in every dimension of life, and within relationships of the person to other people and to God.

Exodus 15:26 (NIV)

He said, **"If you listen carefully to the LORD your God and do what is right in his eyes if you pay attention to his commands and keep all his decrees, I will not bring on the Egyptians, for I am the Lord, who heals."**

Jesus' **Definition** - Abide in Christ; God will heal broken hearts and bind up wounds.

Keys to **Healing**:

1. Figure out what needs restoring. Take time to think.

2. Renew your mind and spirit. Mediate. Renewing the spirit will ultimately renew the body.

3. Spend time with your spiritual, heavenly Father. Educate yourself.

4. Believe in Christ Jesus. Have morals and standards.

5. Make healthy choices. (Healthy choices aren't always about eating right!) Healthy life decisions will lead to healthy eating habits.

6. Stay consistent with daily techniques and journaling.

7. Incorporate a daily prayer life with meaning and understanding.

Healing will release any toxic spirits; healing will create in you a clean and righteous heart; healing will allow you to receive what God has intended for your life. Healing will allow the gift of forgiveness to become a routine check throughout your life. Healing will restore what was lost or caused pain, grief, stress, disappointment, and any feelings of heartache. Healing will give you peace more often than you were accustomed to.

1 Peter 2:24 (NIV) **He himself bore our sins in his body on the cross, so that we might die of sins and live for righteousness. By his wounds you have been healed.**

Healing has power!

Journal page

6 Consistency

How could we ever achieve dreams, goals, success, or all that God has for us? Suppose we have not figured out how to stay dedicated, committed, accountable, focused, or sustain positive thoughts. How can we expect to be all that we want to be the most efficient and effective in life?

If we think about consistency, we all have it in us from childhood to adulthood.

Newborns make a consistent cry when they're hungry, wet, or not feeling well.

Infants learn to sit up, hold a bottle, crawl, etc. They repeated the action until finally, they did it on their own.

Toddlers and school-aged children learn to walk, run, and speak in the same way.

Adolescents repeatedly make good judgments and excel or repeatedly make bad judgments and fail.

Adults know wrong from right but choose to repeat bad choices and use excuses throughout life.

Being consistent means dedicating yourself to your goals and staying focused on the things and activities to achieve your goals.

Consistency requires a long-term commitment from you and involves sustained effort in repeating actions until you achieve your goals. Someone who is consistent always behaves in the same way, maintains the same attitudes towards people or things, or achieves the same level of success or lack of success in something.

Consistency leads to momentum.

The more consistently you do something, the easier it becomes and the more momentum you build up. Eventually, what was once a struggle becomes a habit, and habits are hard to break. That's why consistency is so important—it is the key to making lasting change.

Definition of consistency - agreement or harmony of parts or features to one another or a whole, dedicating yourself to your goals and staying focused on the things and activities to achieve your goals.

Biblical definition -To abide, to stay in a given place. For believers, it means maintaining **an unbroken** relationship with God.

Jesus' definition – Faith over experiences.

Galatians 6:9 (ESV) **And let us not grow weary of doing good, for in due season we will reap if we do not give up.**

John 2:6 (NKJV) **He who says he abides in him ought himself also to walk just as he walked.**

Make time for the Word of God and prayer every day. If you are too busy, decide to schedule your time with the Word or rearrange some things on your schedule. But make sure God's Word is incorporated daily.

Keys to **Consistency**:

1. Isolate from people with negative energy and stop trying to accomplish too many goals at one time.

2. Focus on one goal until completion.

3. Fight your emotions, understand what's happening in real time, deal with that emotion, and move on. Don't hold on to that emotion for too long.

4. Forgive your failures and move on.

5. Demonstrate a high level of integrity and loyalty.

6. Identify who you are.

7. Pray – John 15:4 (ESV) **Abide in me, and I in you. As the branch cannot bear fruit of itself, unless it abides in the vine, neither can you, unless you abide in me.**

~ Consistency leads to habits. ~

~ Consistency is not giving up. ~

The difference between successful people and those who give up on their goals is consistency.

John Maxwell says, "Small disciplines repeated with consistency every day lead to great achievements gained slowly over time."

Maxwell, J (2012). The 15 Invaluable Laws of Growth

Journal page

7 Balance

Balancing made this chapter come alive. Life is so unbalanced, but that makes you search for God even more. The way God balances life out for us should determine how we walk around in life. If we think about the power of control, how God is in control, and how he's able to control the world, it is all a part of a balanced life. Life will always throw a monkey wrench at times, but the ability to take control of what's to come will help us escape the agony of a mental and physical breakdown.

Definition of balance - keep or put something in a steady position so that it does not fall.

Biblical definition - loving God and enjoying earthly blessings while not putting any hope in them, while balance is a system of justice and fair dealings versus wrongs.

Jesus Definition— Scales and balances are to be used with fairness and equity also applying fairness and equity to God's way of life.

Keys To **Balance**:

1. Create a schedule and put yourself at the top of that list.

2. Prioritize.

3. Have an open ear and heart to situations.

4. Surround yourself with meaningful relationships.

5. Connect yourself with good-energy people and activities.

6. Rest well and eat healthy.

7. Pray for yourself and others.

~ Proverbs 11:1 (ESV)~

A false balance is an abomination to the Lord, but a just weight is His delight.

J ournal page

Epilogue

Let the end of this publication be the Beginning to a new start of You getting more joy out of life, being able to be in control of what happens in your life. Let's gain control of constant positivity. After reading, meditating, and now gaining, understanding, wisdom and knowledge let's start LIVING y'all!!!!!!! Build on Hope and not Hopelessness, Keep fighting the temptations, negative thinking, overthinking, and most importantly the devil and his soldiers.

You ask how do I fight back?

Thank you for asking- with God's word, obeying his word, faith in Jesus the Christ and Trusting in God always.

BreW